50 Premium Delicious Pizza Recipes

By: Kelly Johnson

Table of Contents

- Margherita Pizza
- Pepperoni and Sausage Supreme
- Four Cheese Delight
- Truffle Mushroom Pizza
- BBQ Chicken Pizza
- Hawaiian Classic
- Pesto Chicken and Sun-Dried Tomato
- Spinach and Artichoke Pizza
- Buffalo Chicken Pizza
- Fig and Prosciutto Pizza
- Meat Lovers Pizza
- Roasted Vegetable Pizza
- Mediterranean Veggie Pizza
- Shrimp Scampi Pizza
- White Pizza with Ricotta and Spinach
- Margherita with Balsamic Glaze
- Smoked Salmon and Cream Cheese Pizza
- Eggplant Parmesan Pizza
- Breakfast Pizza with Eggs and Bacon
- Philly Cheesesteak Pizza
- Goat Cheese and Beetroot Pizza
- Pear and Gorgonzola Pizza
- Italian Sausage and Peppers Pizza
- Caprese Pizza with Fresh Basil
- Vegan Mediterranean Pizza
- Mushroom and Truffle Oil Pizza
- Lobster and Garlic Butter Pizza
- Roasted Garlic and Goat Cheese Pizza
- BBQ Pulled Pork Pizza
- Spicy Sriracha Chicken Pizza
- Meatball and Ricotta Pizza
- Roasted Red Pepper and Feta Pizza
- Lobster and Mango Salsa Pizza
- Bacon and Brussels Sprout Pizza
- Zaatar and Cheese Pizza

- Grilled Chicken Caesar Pizza
- Sweet Potato and Kale Pizza
- Fig, Prosciutto, and Arugula Pizza
- Tandoori Chicken Pizza
- Spicy Thai Chicken Pizza
- Clam and Garlic White Sauce Pizza
- Buffalo Cauliflower Pizza
- Cucumber and Dill Pizza
- BBQ Brisket Pizza
- Chicken Alfredo Pizza
- Butternut Squash and Sage Pizza
- Apple and Bacon Pizza
- Black Bean and Corn Pizza
- Caramelized Onion and Brie Pizza
- Blue Cheese and Pear Pizza

Margherita Pizza

Ingredients:

- **1 pizza dough** (store-bought or homemade)
- **1/2 cup pizza sauce**
- **8 oz fresh mozzarella cheese**, sliced
- **1/4 cup fresh basil leaves**
- **Olive oil** (for drizzling)
- **Salt and pepper** (to taste)

Instructions:

1. Preheat oven to 475°F (245°C).
2. Roll out the pizza dough on a lightly floured surface to your desired thickness.
3. Spread pizza sauce evenly over the dough.
4. Arrange slices of fresh mozzarella on top of the sauce.
5. Season with salt and pepper and drizzle with a little olive oil.
6. Bake for 10-12 minutes or until the crust is golden and the cheese is melted and bubbly.
7. Remove from the oven and top with fresh basil leaves before serving.

Pepperoni and Sausage Supreme

Ingredients:

- **1 pizza dough** (store-bought or homemade)
- **1/2 cup pizza sauce**
- **1/2 cup mozzarella cheese**, shredded
- **1/2 cup Italian sausage**, cooked and crumbled
- **1/4 cup pepperoni slices**
- **1/4 cup green bell pepper**, sliced
- **1/4 cup red onion**, sliced
- **1/4 teaspoon dried oregano**

Instructions:

1. Preheat oven to 475°F (245°C).
2. Roll out the pizza dough and place on a baking sheet or pizza stone.
3. Spread the pizza sauce over the dough.
4. Sprinkle mozzarella cheese evenly on top.
5. Add cooked sausage, pepperoni, green bell pepper, and red onion.
6. Season with dried oregano.
7. Bake for 10-12 minutes or until the cheese is melted and the crust is golden brown.

Four Cheese Delight

Ingredients:

- **1 pizza dough** (store-bought or homemade)
- **1/2 cup pizza sauce**
- **1/4 cup mozzarella cheese**, shredded
- **1/4 cup cheddar cheese**, shredded
- **1/4 cup Parmesan cheese**, grated
- **1/4 cup ricotta cheese**
- **Fresh basil** (optional)

Instructions:

1. Preheat oven to 475°F (245°C).
2. Roll out the pizza dough and transfer to a baking sheet or pizza stone.
3. Spread pizza sauce evenly on the dough.
4. Sprinkle mozzarella, cheddar, and Parmesan cheeses on top.
5. Dot with spoonfuls of ricotta cheese.
6. Bake for 10-12 minutes or until the crust is golden and the cheese is bubbly.
7. Garnish with fresh basil if desired and serve.

Truffle Mushroom Pizza

Ingredients:

- **1 pizza dough** (store-bought or homemade)
- **1/2 cup pizza sauce**
- **1/2 cup mozzarella cheese**, shredded
- **1/4 cup Parmesan cheese**, grated
- **1 cup mushrooms**, sliced (such as cremini or button mushrooms)
- **1 tablespoon truffle oil**
- **Fresh parsley**, chopped (for garnish)
- **Salt and pepper** (to taste)

Instructions:

1. Preheat oven to 475°F (245°C).
2. Roll out the pizza dough on a floured surface.
3. Spread a thin layer of pizza sauce on the dough.
4. Sprinkle mozzarella and Parmesan cheeses evenly over the sauce.
5. Sauté the mushrooms in a pan with a little olive oil until tender, then scatter them over the pizza.
6. Drizzle with truffle oil and season with salt and pepper.
7. Bake for 10-12 minutes until the cheese is melted and the crust is golden.
8. Garnish with fresh parsley and serve.

BBQ Chicken Pizza

Ingredients:

- **1 pizza dough** (store-bought or homemade)
- **1/2 cup BBQ sauce**
- **1/2 cup cooked chicken**, shredded
- **1/4 cup red onion**, thinly sliced
- **1/2 cup mozzarella cheese**, shredded
- **1/4 cup cilantro**, chopped

Instructions:

1. Preheat oven to 475°F (245°C).
2. Roll out the pizza dough and transfer to a baking sheet or pizza stone.
3. Spread BBQ sauce over the dough, leaving a border for the crust.
4. Top with shredded chicken, red onion, and mozzarella cheese.
5. Bake for 10-12 minutes or until the cheese is bubbly and the crust is golden.
6. Remove from the oven and sprinkle with fresh cilantro before serving.

Hawaiian Classic

Ingredients:

- **1 pizza dough** (store-bought or homemade)
- **1/2 cup pizza sauce**
- **1/2 cup mozzarella cheese**, shredded
- **1/2 cup ham**, diced
- **1/2 cup pineapple chunks**, drained

Instructions:

1. Preheat oven to 475°F (245°C).
2. Roll out the pizza dough and place on a baking sheet or pizza stone.
3. Spread pizza sauce over the dough.
4. Sprinkle mozzarella cheese evenly over the sauce.
5. Add ham and pineapple chunks.
6. Bake for 10-12 minutes or until the cheese is melted and the crust is golden.
7. Serve immediately.

Pesto Chicken and Sun-Dried Tomato

Ingredients:

- **1 pizza dough** (store-bought or homemade)
- **1/4 cup pesto sauce**
- **1/2 cup cooked chicken**, shredded
- **1/4 cup sun-dried tomatoes**, chopped
- **1/2 cup mozzarella cheese**, shredded
- **1 tablespoon pine nuts** (optional)

Instructions:

1. Preheat oven to 475°F (245°C).
2. Roll out the pizza dough and transfer to a baking sheet or pizza stone.
3. Spread pesto sauce over the dough.
4. Top with shredded chicken, sun-dried tomatoes, and mozzarella cheese.
5. Optionally, sprinkle pine nuts over the pizza.
6. Bake for 10-12 minutes until the cheese is melted and bubbly.

Spinach and Artichoke Pizza

Ingredients:

- **1 pizza dough** (store-bought or homemade)
- **1/2 cup pizza sauce**
- **1/2 cup mozzarella cheese**, shredded
- **1/4 cup Parmesan cheese**, grated
- **1/2 cup spinach**, fresh or frozen (thawed and drained)
- **1/2 cup artichoke hearts**, chopped (canned or jarred)

Instructions:

1. Preheat oven to 475°F (245°C).
2. Roll out the pizza dough and place on a baking sheet or pizza stone.
3. Spread a thin layer of pizza sauce on the dough.
4. Top with mozzarella and Parmesan cheeses.
5. Scatter spinach and artichoke hearts evenly over the cheese.
6. Bake for 10-12 minutes until the cheese is melted and bubbly.

Buffalo Chicken Pizza

Ingredients:

- **1 pizza dough** (store-bought or homemade)
- **1/4 cup buffalo sauce**
- **1/2 cup cooked chicken**, shredded
- **1/2 cup mozzarella cheese**, shredded
- **1/4 cup blue cheese**, crumbled
- **Celery** (optional, for garnish)

Instructions:

1. Preheat oven to 475°F (245°C).
2. Roll out the pizza dough and place it on a baking sheet or pizza stone.
3. Spread buffalo sauce over the dough.
4. Add shredded chicken and mozzarella cheese.
5. Bake for 10-12 minutes, then remove from the oven and sprinkle with crumbled blue cheese.
6. Optionally, garnish with fresh celery and serve.

Fig and Prosciutto Pizza

Ingredients:

- **1 pizza dough** (store-bought or homemade)
- **1/2 cup olive tapenade** or **fig jam**
- **4 oz prosciutto**, thinly sliced
- **1/2 cup mozzarella cheese**, shredded
- **1/4 cup goat cheese** (optional)
- **Arugula** (for garnish)
- **Balsamic glaze** (for drizzling)
- **Olive oil** (for drizzling)
- **Fresh ground black pepper** (to taste)

Instructions:

1. Preheat oven to 475°F (245°C).
2. Roll out the pizza dough and transfer to a baking sheet or pizza stone.
3. Spread olive tapenade or fig jam evenly over the dough.
4. Sprinkle mozzarella cheese and dot with goat cheese.
5. Add prosciutto slices evenly over the cheese.
6. Bake for 10-12 minutes or until the crust is golden and the cheese is melted.
7. Remove from the oven, drizzle with olive oil and balsamic glaze, and top with fresh arugula.
8. Slice and serve immediately.

Meat Lovers Pizza

Ingredients:

- **1 pizza dough** (store-bought or homemade)
- **1/2 cup pizza sauce**
- **1/2 cup mozzarella cheese**, shredded
- **1/4 cup cooked sausage**, crumbled
- **1/4 cup pepperoni slices**
- **1/4 cup cooked bacon**, crumbled
- **1/4 cup ham**, diced
- **1/4 cup ground beef**, cooked and crumbled
- **Dried oregano** (optional, for garnish)

Instructions:

1. Preheat oven to 475°F (245°C).
2. Roll out the pizza dough and place on a baking sheet or pizza stone.
3. Spread pizza sauce over the dough.
4. Sprinkle mozzarella cheese evenly over the sauce.
5. Layer on all the meats: sausage, pepperoni, bacon, ham, and ground beef.
6. Bake for 10-12 minutes or until the cheese is bubbly and the crust is golden.
7. Optionally, garnish with dried oregano and serve.

Roasted Vegetable Pizza

Ingredients:

- **1 pizza dough** (store-bought or homemade)
- **1/2 cup pizza sauce** or **olive tapenade**
- **1/2 cup mozzarella cheese**, shredded
- **1/4 cup bell peppers**, sliced
- **1/4 cup zucchini**, thinly sliced
- **1/4 cup red onion**, sliced
- **1/4 cup cherry tomatoes**, halved
- **1/4 cup mushrooms**, sliced
- **Olive oil** (for drizzling)
- **Fresh basil leaves** (for garnish)
- **Salt and pepper** (to taste)

Instructions:

1. Preheat oven to 475°F (245°C).
2. Roll out the pizza dough and place on a baking sheet or pizza stone.
3. Spread pizza sauce or olive tapenade evenly over the dough.
4. Sprinkle mozzarella cheese evenly on top.
5. Arrange the roasted vegetables—bell peppers, zucchini, red onion, tomatoes, and mushrooms—over the cheese.
6. Drizzle with olive oil and season with salt and pepper.
7. Bake for 10-12 minutes until the cheese is melted and bubbly.
8. Garnish with fresh basil leaves before serving.

Mediterranean Veggie Pizza

Ingredients:

- **1 pizza dough** (store-bought or homemade)
- **1/2 cup hummus** (as sauce)
- **1/2 cup mozzarella cheese**, shredded
- **1/4 cup kalamata olives**, pitted and sliced
- **1/4 cup artichoke hearts**, chopped
- **1/4 cup red onion**, thinly sliced
- **1/4 cup cherry tomatoes**, halved
- **Feta cheese**, crumbled
- **Fresh oregano or basil** (for garnish)

Instructions:

1. Preheat oven to 475°F (245°C).
2. Roll out the pizza dough and place on a baking sheet or pizza stone.
3. Spread hummus evenly as the base on the dough.
4. Sprinkle mozzarella cheese evenly over the hummus.
5. Add olives, artichoke hearts, red onion, cherry tomatoes, and feta cheese on top.
6. Bake for 10-12 minutes or until the cheese is melted and the crust is golden.
7. Garnish with fresh oregano or basil and serve.

Shrimp Scampi Pizza

Ingredients:

- **1 pizza dough** (store-bought or homemade)
- **1/4 cup garlic butter** (melted)
- **1/2 cup mozzarella cheese**, shredded
- **1/2 lb shrimp**, peeled and deveined
- **1/4 cup Parmesan cheese**, grated
- **Fresh parsley**, chopped
- **Lemon wedges** (for serving)
- **Red pepper flakes** (optional)

Instructions:

1. Preheat oven to 475°F (245°C).
2. Roll out the pizza dough and transfer to a baking sheet or pizza stone.
3. Brush the dough with melted garlic butter.
4. Sprinkle mozzarella cheese evenly over the dough.
5. Arrange the shrimp evenly over the cheese.
6. Sprinkle Parmesan cheese over the top.
7. Bake for 10-12 minutes until the cheese is bubbly and shrimp are cooked through.
8. Garnish with fresh parsley and serve with lemon wedges. Optionally, add red pepper flakes for a bit of spice.

White Pizza with Ricotta and Spinach

Ingredients:

- **1 pizza dough** (store-bought or homemade)
- **1/2 cup ricotta cheese**
- **1/2 cup mozzarella cheese**, shredded
- **1/2 cup Parmesan cheese**, grated
- **1 cup fresh spinach** (or frozen, thawed and drained)
- **1 garlic clove**, minced
- **Olive oil** (for drizzling)
- **Salt and pepper** (to taste)

Instructions:

1. Preheat oven to 475°F (245°C).
2. Roll out the pizza dough and place on a baking sheet or pizza stone.
3. In a bowl, mix ricotta, mozzarella, Parmesan, and minced garlic.
4. Spread the cheese mixture evenly over the dough.
5. Top with fresh spinach and drizzle with olive oil.
6. Bake for 10-12 minutes until the crust is golden and the cheese is melted.
7. Season with salt and pepper and serve.

Margherita with Balsamic Glaze

Ingredients:

- **1 pizza dough** (store-bought or homemade)
- **1/2 cup pizza sauce**
- **8 oz fresh mozzarella cheese**, sliced
- **Fresh basil leaves**
- **Balsamic glaze** (for drizzling)
- **Olive oil** (for drizzling)
- **Salt and pepper** (to taste)

Instructions:

1. Preheat oven to 475°F (245°C).
2. Roll out the pizza dough and transfer to a baking sheet or pizza stone.
3. Spread pizza sauce evenly over the dough.
4. Arrange fresh mozzarella slices on top of the sauce.
5. Season with salt and pepper, and drizzle with a little olive oil.
6. Bake for 10-12 minutes until the cheese is melted and bubbly.
7. Remove from the oven and drizzle with balsamic glaze and garnish with fresh basil leaves before serving.

Smoked Salmon and Cream Cheese Pizza

Ingredients:

- **1 pizza dough** (store-bought or homemade)
- **1/4 cup cream cheese**, softened
- **1/2 cup mozzarella cheese**, shredded
- **4 oz smoked salmon**, sliced
- **1/4 red onion**, thinly sliced
- **Capers** (optional)
- **Fresh dill** (for garnish)
- **Lemon wedges** (for serving)

Instructions:

1. Preheat oven to 475°F (245°C).
2. Roll out the pizza dough and transfer to a baking sheet or pizza stone.
3. Spread a thin layer of cream cheese on the dough.
4. Sprinkle mozzarella cheese evenly over the cream cheese.
5. Bake for 8-10 minutes until the crust is golden and the cheese is melted.
6. Remove from the oven and top with smoked salmon, red onion, and capers (if using).
7. Garnish with fresh dill and serve with lemon wedges.

Eggplant Parmesan Pizza

Ingredients:

- **1 pizza dough** (store-bought or homemade)
- **1/2 cup marinara sauce**
- **1/2 cup mozzarella cheese**, shredded
- **1/4 cup Parmesan cheese**, grated
- **1 small eggplant**, sliced and breaded
- **Olive oil** (for frying)
- **Fresh basil leaves** (for garnish)
- **Salt and pepper** (to taste)

Instructions:

1. Preheat oven to 475°F (245°C).
2. Roll out the pizza dough and transfer to a baking sheet or pizza stone.
3. Spread marinara sauce evenly over the dough.
4. Sprinkle mozzarella and Parmesan cheese on top.
5. Pan-fry the breaded eggplant slices in olive oil until golden brown and crispy.
6. Arrange the fried eggplant slices on top of the pizza.
7. Bake for 10-12 minutes or until the cheese is melted and the crust is golden.
8. Garnish with fresh basil, salt, and pepper, then serve.

Breakfast Pizza with Eggs and Bacon

Ingredients:

- **1 pizza dough** (store-bought or homemade)
- **1/2 cup pizza sauce** or **cream cheese** (as base)
- **1/2 cup mozzarella cheese**, shredded
- **4 eggs**
- **4 slices cooked bacon**, crumbled
- **Green onions**, chopped (for garnish)
- **Fresh parsley** (optional)
- **Salt and pepper** (to taste)

Instructions:

1. Preheat oven to 475°F (245°C).
2. Roll out the pizza dough and transfer to a baking sheet or pizza stone.
3. Spread pizza sauce or cream cheese on the dough as the base.
4. Sprinkle mozzarella cheese over the sauce.
5. Crack eggs onto the pizza, leaving space between each.
6. Add crumbled bacon over the eggs.
7. Bake for 10-12 minutes or until the eggs are cooked to your liking and the cheese is melted.
8. Garnish with chopped green onions and fresh parsley, then serve.

Philly Cheesesteak Pizza

Ingredients:

- **1 pizza dough** (store-bought or homemade)
- **1/2 cup pizza sauce** or **ranch dressing** (as base)
- **1/2 cup mozzarella cheese**, shredded
- **1/2 cup provolone cheese**, shredded
- **1/2 cup cooked steak**, thinly sliced
- **1/4 cup onions**, thinly sliced
- **1/4 cup bell peppers**, thinly sliced
- **Olive oil** (for sautéing)
- **Salt and pepper** (to taste)

Instructions:

1. Preheat oven to 475°F (245°C).
2. Roll out the pizza dough and transfer to a baking sheet or pizza stone.
3. Spread pizza sauce or ranch dressing over the dough.
4. Sprinkle mozzarella and provolone cheese over the sauce.
5. Sauté onions and bell peppers in olive oil until softened.
6. Top the pizza with sautéed onions, peppers, and cooked steak.
7. Bake for 10-12 minutes until the cheese is melted and the crust is golden.
8. Season with salt and pepper and serve.

Goat Cheese and Beetroot Pizza

Ingredients:

- **1 pizza dough** (store-bought or homemade)
- **1/2 cup pizza sauce** or **balsamic glaze**
- **1/2 cup goat cheese**, crumbled
- **1/2 cup mozzarella cheese**, shredded
- **1/4 cup roasted beetroot**, sliced
- **Fresh arugula** (for garnish)
- **Walnuts** (optional, for garnish)
- **Olive oil** (for drizzling)

Instructions:

1. Preheat oven to 475°F (245°C).
2. Roll out the pizza dough and transfer to a baking sheet or pizza stone.
3. Spread pizza sauce or drizzle balsamic glaze over the dough.
4. Sprinkle mozzarella and goat cheese evenly over the sauce.
5. Arrange roasted beetroot slices on top.
6. Bake for 10-12 minutes or until the cheese is melted and the crust is golden.
7. Garnish with fresh arugula, walnuts, and a drizzle of olive oil before serving.

Pear and Gorgonzola Pizza

Ingredients:

- **1 pizza dough** (store-bought or homemade)
- **1/2 cup mozzarella cheese**, shredded
- **1/4 cup Gorgonzola cheese**, crumbled
- **1 pear**, thinly sliced
- **Walnuts** (optional, for garnish)
- **Honey** (for drizzling)
- **Arugula** (for garnish)
- **Olive oil** (for drizzling)

Instructions:

1. Preheat oven to 475°F (245°C).
2. Roll out the pizza dough and transfer to a baking sheet or pizza stone.
3. Sprinkle mozzarella cheese evenly over the dough.
4. Add crumbled Gorgonzola cheese and pear slices.
5. Bake for 10-12 minutes or until the cheese is melted and the crust is golden.
6. Drizzle with honey and garnish with fresh arugula and walnuts before serving.

Italian Sausage and Peppers Pizza

Ingredients:

- **1 pizza dough** (store-bought or homemade)
- **1/2 cup pizza sauce**
- **1/2 cup mozzarella cheese**, shredded
- **2 Italian sausages**, cooked and crumbled
- **1/4 cup bell peppers**, sliced
- **1/4 cup onions**, sliced
- **Olive oil** (for sautéing)
- **Fresh parsley** (optional, for garnish)
- **Salt and pepper** (to taste)

Instructions:

1. Preheat oven to 475°F (245°C).
2. Roll out the pizza dough and transfer to a baking sheet or pizza stone.
3. Spread pizza sauce evenly over the dough.
4. Sprinkle mozzarella cheese evenly on top.
5. Sauté bell peppers and onions in olive oil until softened.
6. Top the pizza with cooked sausage, sautéed peppers, and onions.
7. Bake for 10-12 minutes or until the cheese is melted and the crust is golden.
8. Garnish with fresh parsley and season with salt and pepper before serving.

Caprese Pizza with Fresh Basil

Ingredients:

- **1 pizza dough** (store-bought or homemade)
- **1/2 cup pizza sauce** or **pesto**
- **1/2 cup mozzarella cheese**, shredded
- **1/2 cup fresh mozzarella**, sliced
- **1/4 cup cherry tomatoes**, halved
- **Fresh basil leaves** (for garnish)
- **Balsamic glaze** (for drizzling)
- **Olive oil** (for drizzling)

Instructions:

1. Preheat oven to 475°F (245°C).
2. Roll out the pizza dough and transfer to a baking sheet or pizza stone.
3. Spread pizza sauce or pesto evenly over the dough.
4. Sprinkle shredded mozzarella cheese on top and arrange fresh mozzarella slices.
5. Add halved cherry tomatoes over the mozzarella.
6. Bake for 10-12 minutes until the cheese is melted and the crust is golden.
7. Garnish with fresh basil, drizzle with balsamic glaze and olive oil before serving.

Vegan Mediterranean Pizza

Ingredients:

- **1 pizza dough** (store-bought or homemade)
- **1/2 cup hummus** (as sauce)
- **1/2 cup vegan mozzarella cheese**, shredded
- **1/4 cup black olives**, pitted and sliced
- **1/4 cup artichoke hearts**, chopped
- **1/4 cup red onion**, sliced
- **1/4 cup cherry tomatoes**, halved
- **Fresh oregano** (for garnish)

Instructions:

1. Preheat oven to 475°F (245°C).
2. Roll out the pizza dough and transfer to a baking sheet or pizza stone.
3. Spread hummus evenly over the dough.
4. Sprinkle vegan mozzarella cheese on top.
5. Add olives, artichokes, red onion, and tomatoes over the cheese.
6. Bake for 10-12 minutes until the cheese is melted and the crust is golden.
7. Garnish with fresh oregano and serve.

Mushroom and Truffle Oil Pizza

Ingredients:

- **1 pizza dough** (store-bought or homemade)
- **1/2 cup olive oil** (for brushing)
- **1/2 cup mozzarella cheese**, shredded
- **1/2 cup mixed mushrooms**, sliced
- **1/4 cup Parmesan cheese**, grated
- **Truffle oil** (for drizzling)
- **Fresh thyme** (for garnish)
- **Salt and pepper** (to taste)

Instructions:

1. Preheat oven to 475°F (245°C).
2. Roll out the pizza dough and transfer to a baking sheet or pizza stone.
3. Brush the dough lightly with olive oil.
4. Sprinkle mozzarella cheese evenly over the dough.
5. Arrange sliced mushrooms over the cheese.
6. Sprinkle with Parmesan cheese, salt, and pepper.
7. Bake for 10-12 minutes until the cheese is melted and the crust is golden.
8. Drizzle with truffle oil and garnish with fresh thyme before serving.

Lobster and Garlic Butter Pizza

Ingredients:

- **1 pizza dough** (store-bought or homemade)
- **1/2 cup garlic butter** (melted)
- **1/2 cup mozzarella cheese**, shredded
- **1/2 cup cooked lobster meat**, chopped
- **1/4 cup fresh parsley**, chopped
- **1/4 cup Parmesan cheese**, grated
- **Fresh lemon juice** (optional, for drizzling)
- **Olive oil** (for brushing)

Instructions:

1. Preheat oven to 475°F (245°C).
2. Roll out the pizza dough and transfer to a baking sheet or pizza stone.
3. Brush the dough with olive oil, then spread the melted garlic butter evenly over the dough.
4. Sprinkle mozzarella and Parmesan cheese over the garlic butter.
5. Distribute chopped lobster meat over the cheese.
6. Bake for 10-12 minutes until the cheese is melted and the crust is golden.
7. Garnish with fresh parsley and a squeeze of lemon juice before serving.

Roasted Garlic and Goat Cheese Pizza

Ingredients:

- **1 pizza dough** (store-bought or homemade)
- **1/2 cup olive oil** (for brushing)
- **1/4 cup roasted garlic** (mashed)
- **1/2 cup goat cheese**, crumbled
- **1/2 cup mozzarella cheese**, shredded
- **Fresh rosemary** (for garnish)
- **Salt and pepper** (to taste)

Instructions:

1. Preheat oven to 475°F (245°C).
2. Roll out the pizza dough and transfer to a baking sheet or pizza stone.
3. Brush the dough lightly with olive oil.
4. Spread roasted garlic evenly over the dough.
5. Sprinkle mozzarella cheese and crumbled goat cheese on top.
6. Bake for 10-12 minutes until the cheese is melted and the crust is golden.
7. Garnish with fresh rosemary, salt, and pepper before serving.

BBQ Pulled Pork Pizza

Ingredients:

- **1 pizza dough** (store-bought or homemade)
- **1/2 cup BBQ sauce**
- **1/2 cup mozzarella cheese**, shredded
- **1/2 cup cooked pulled pork**
- **1/4 cup red onions**, thinly sliced
- **1/4 cup cilantro**, chopped
- **1/4 cup cheddar cheese**, shredded

Instructions:

1. Preheat oven to 475°F (245°C).
2. Roll out the pizza dough and transfer to a baking sheet or pizza stone.
3. Spread BBQ sauce evenly over the dough.
4. Sprinkle mozzarella and cheddar cheese over the sauce.
5. Add pulled pork and red onions on top.
6. Bake for 10-12 minutes until the cheese is melted and the crust is golden.
7. Garnish with chopped cilantro before serving.

Spicy Sriracha Chicken Pizza

Ingredients:

- **1 pizza dough** (store-bought or homemade)
- **1/4 cup Sriracha sauce**
- **1/2 cup mozzarella cheese**, shredded
- **1/2 cup cooked chicken**, shredded
- **1/4 cup red onions**, thinly sliced
- **1/4 cup bell peppers**, sliced
- **Fresh cilantro** (for garnish)
- **Lime wedges** (for serving)

Instructions:

1. Preheat oven to 475°F (245°C).
2. Roll out the pizza dough and transfer to a baking sheet or pizza stone.
3. Spread Sriracha sauce evenly over the dough.
4. Sprinkle mozzarella cheese over the sauce.
5. Add shredded chicken, red onions, and bell peppers on top.
6. Bake for 10-12 minutes until the cheese is melted and the crust is golden.
7. Garnish with fresh cilantro and serve with lime wedges.

Meatball and Ricotta Pizza

Ingredients:

- **1 pizza dough** (store-bought or homemade)
- **1/2 cup pizza sauce**
- **1/2 cup mozzarella cheese**, shredded
- **1/4 cup ricotta cheese**
- **8-10 small meatballs**, cooked and halved
- **Fresh basil leaves** (for garnish)
- **Parmesan cheese**, grated (for garnish)

Instructions:

1. Preheat oven to 475°F (245°C).
2. Roll out the pizza dough and transfer to a baking sheet or pizza stone.
3. Spread pizza sauce evenly over the dough.
4. Sprinkle mozzarella cheese over the sauce.
5. Add meatball halves and dollops of ricotta cheese on top.
6. Bake for 10-12 minutes until the cheese is melted and the crust is golden.
7. Garnish with fresh basil and Parmesan cheese before serving.

Roasted Red Pepper and Feta Pizza

Ingredients:

- **1 pizza dough** (store-bought or homemade)
- **1/2 cup pizza sauce**
- **1/2 cup mozzarella cheese**, shredded
- **1/4 cup roasted red peppers**, sliced
- **1/4 cup feta cheese**, crumbled
- **Fresh basil** (for garnish)
- **Olive oil** (for drizzling)

Instructions:

1. Preheat oven to 475°F (245°C).
2. Roll out the pizza dough and transfer to a baking sheet or pizza stone.
3. Spread pizza sauce evenly over the dough.
4. Sprinkle mozzarella cheese over the sauce.
5. Add roasted red peppers and crumbled feta cheese on top.
6. Bake for 10-12 minutes until the cheese is melted and the crust is golden.
7. Garnish with fresh basil and drizzle with olive oil before serving.

Lobster and Mango Salsa Pizza

Ingredients:

- **1 pizza dough** (store-bought or homemade)
- **1/2 cup pizza sauce** or **garlic butter**
- **1/2 cup mozzarella cheese**, shredded
- **1/2 cup cooked lobster meat**, chopped
- **1/4 cup mango salsa**
- **Fresh cilantro**, chopped (for garnish)

Instructions:

1. Preheat oven to 475°F (245°C).
2. Roll out the pizza dough and transfer to a baking sheet or pizza stone.
3. Spread pizza sauce or garlic butter evenly over the dough.
4. Sprinkle mozzarella cheese over the sauce.
5. Add chopped lobster meat and top with mango salsa.
6. Bake for 10-12 minutes until the cheese is melted and the crust is golden.
7. Garnish with fresh cilantro before serving.

Bacon and Brussels Sprout Pizza

Ingredients:

- **1 pizza dough** (store-bought or homemade)
- **1/2 cup mozzarella cheese**, shredded
- **1/4 cup Parmesan cheese**, grated
- **1/2 cup cooked bacon**, crumbled
- **1/2 cup Brussels sprouts**, thinly sliced
- **Olive oil** (for drizzling)
- **Salt and pepper** (to taste)

Instructions:

1. Preheat oven to 475°F (245°C).
2. Roll out the pizza dough and transfer to a baking sheet or pizza stone.
3. Sprinkle mozzarella cheese and Parmesan cheese over the dough.
4. Distribute crumbled bacon and sliced Brussels sprouts over the cheese.
5. Drizzle with olive oil and season with salt and pepper.
6. Bake for 10-12 minutes until the cheese is melted and the crust is golden.

Zaatar and Cheese Pizza

Ingredients:

- **1 pizza dough** (store-bought or homemade)
- **1/4 cup olive oil**
- **2 tbsp zaatar spice mix**
- **1/2 cup mozzarella cheese**, shredded
- **1/4 cup feta cheese**, crumbled
- **Fresh parsley** (for garnish)

Instructions:

1. Preheat oven to 475°F (245°C).
2. Roll out the pizza dough and transfer to a baking sheet or pizza stone.
3. Brush the dough lightly with olive oil.
4. Sprinkle zaatar spice mix evenly over the dough.
5. Add mozzarella cheese and crumbled feta cheese on top.
6. Bake for 10-12 minutes until the cheese is melted and the crust is golden.
7. Garnish with fresh parsley before serving.

Grilled Chicken Caesar Pizza

Ingredients:

- **1 pizza dough** (store-bought or homemade)
- **1/2 cup Caesar dressing**
- **1/2 cup mozzarella cheese**, shredded
- **1/2 cup grilled chicken**, sliced
- **1/4 cup Parmesan cheese**, grated
- **Romaine lettuce**, chopped (for topping after baking)
- **Fresh black pepper** (for garnish)
- **Lemon wedges** (optional)

Instructions:

1. Preheat oven to 475°F (245°C).
2. Roll out the pizza dough and transfer to a baking sheet or pizza stone.
3. Spread Caesar dressing evenly over the dough.
4. Sprinkle mozzarella cheese over the dressing.
5. Add grilled chicken slices on top.
6. Bake for 10-12 minutes until the cheese is melted and the crust is golden.
7. After baking, top with chopped romaine lettuce, Parmesan cheese, and black pepper. Serve with lemon wedges.

Sweet Potato and Kale Pizza

Ingredients:

- **1 pizza dough** (store-bought or homemade)
- **1/2 cup olive oil**
- **1 cup sweet potato**, roasted and sliced thinly
- **1 cup kale**, torn into small pieces
- **1/2 cup mozzarella cheese**, shredded
- **1/4 cup ricotta cheese**, dollops
- **1 tbsp balsamic glaze** (optional)
- **Fresh thyme** (for garnish)
- **Salt and pepper** (to taste)

Instructions:

1. Preheat oven to 475°F (245°C).
2. Roll out the pizza dough and transfer to a baking sheet or pizza stone.
3. Brush olive oil evenly over the dough.
4. Layer the roasted sweet potato slices, kale, and mozzarella cheese over the dough.
5. Add dollops of ricotta cheese on top.
6. Bake for 10-12 minutes until the cheese is melted and the crust is golden.
7. After baking, drizzle with balsamic glaze and garnish with fresh thyme. Season with salt and pepper.

Fig, Prosciutto, and Arugula Pizza

Ingredients:

- **1 pizza dough** (store-bought or homemade)
- **1/2 cup mozzarella cheese**, shredded
- **1/4 cup goat cheese**, crumbled
- **1/2 cup figs**, sliced
- **4-5 slices prosciutto**
- **1/2 cup arugula** (for topping after baking)
- **Balsamic glaze** (for drizzling)
- **Olive oil** (for brushing)

Instructions:

1. Preheat oven to 475°F (245°C).
2. Roll out the pizza dough and transfer to a baking sheet or pizza stone.
3. Brush the dough with olive oil.
4. Sprinkle mozzarella cheese and crumbled goat cheese over the dough.
5. Arrange sliced figs and prosciutto on top.
6. Bake for 10-12 minutes until the cheese is melted and the crust is golden.
7. After baking, top with fresh arugula and drizzle with balsamic glaze.

Tandoori Chicken Pizza

Ingredients:

- **1 pizza dough** (store-bought or homemade)
- **1/2 cup tandoori sauce**
- **1/2 cup mozzarella cheese**, shredded
- **1/2 cup cooked chicken**, marinated in tandoori sauce and sliced
- **1/4 cup red onion**, thinly sliced
- **1/4 cup cilantro**, chopped
- **1 tbsp yogurt** (optional, for topping after baking)

Instructions:

1. Preheat oven to 475°F (245°C).
2. Roll out the pizza dough and transfer to a baking sheet or pizza stone.
3. Spread tandoori sauce evenly over the dough.
4. Sprinkle mozzarella cheese over the sauce.
5. Add tandoori chicken and red onion slices on top.
6. Bake for 10-12 minutes until the cheese is melted and the crust is golden.
7. After baking, top with fresh cilantro and a dollop of yogurt (optional).

Spicy Thai Chicken Pizza

Ingredients:

- **1 pizza dough** (store-bought or homemade)
- **1/4 cup peanut sauce**
- **1/2 cup mozzarella cheese**, shredded
- **1/2 cup cooked chicken**, sliced
- **1/4 cup bell pepper**, thinly sliced
- **1/4 cup red onion**, thinly sliced
- **1/4 cup carrots**, shredded
- **Fresh cilantro** (for garnish)
- **Crushed peanuts** (optional)

Instructions:

1. Preheat oven to 475°F (245°C).
2. Roll out the pizza dough and transfer to a baking sheet or pizza stone.
3. Spread peanut sauce evenly over the dough.
4. Sprinkle mozzarella cheese over the sauce.
5. Add chicken slices, bell pepper, red onion, and shredded carrots on top.
6. Bake for 10-12 minutes until the cheese is melted and the crust is golden.
7. After baking, garnish with fresh cilantro and crushed peanuts, if desired.

Clam and Garlic White Sauce Pizza

Ingredients:

- **1 pizza dough** (store-bought or homemade)
- **1/2 cup white sauce** (garlic cream sauce)
- **1/2 cup mozzarella cheese**, shredded
- **1/2 cup cooked clams**, chopped
- **1/4 cup garlic**, minced
- **1/4 cup fresh parsley**, chopped
- **Fresh lemon wedges** (optional)

Instructions:

1. Preheat oven to 475°F (245°C).
2. Roll out the pizza dough and transfer to a baking sheet or pizza stone.
3. Spread white sauce evenly over the dough.
4. Sprinkle mozzarella cheese over the sauce.
5. Add chopped clams and minced garlic on top.
6. Bake for 10-12 minutes until the cheese is melted and the crust is golden.
7. After baking, garnish with fresh parsley and serve with lemon wedges.

Buffalo Cauliflower Pizza

Ingredients:

- **1 pizza dough** (store-bought or homemade)
- **1/4 cup buffalo sauce**
- **1/2 cup mozzarella cheese**, shredded
- **1 cup cauliflower florets**, roasted
- **1/4 cup blue cheese**, crumbled
- **Fresh celery leaves** (for garnish)
- **Ranch dressing** (optional, for drizzling)

Instructions:

1. Preheat oven to 475°F (245°C).
2. Roll out the pizza dough and transfer to a baking sheet or pizza stone.
3. Spread buffalo sauce evenly over the dough.
4. Sprinkle mozzarella cheese over the sauce.
5. Add roasted cauliflower florets and crumbled blue cheese on top.
6. Bake for 10-12 minutes until the cheese is melted and the crust is golden.
7. After baking, garnish with fresh celery leaves and drizzle with ranch dressing if desired.

Cucumber and Dill Pizza

Ingredients:

- **1 pizza dough** (store-bought or homemade)
- **1/2 cup cream cheese**, softened
- **1/2 cup mozzarella cheese**, shredded
- **1/4 cup cucumber**, thinly sliced
- **1/4 cup fresh dill**, chopped
- **Lemon zest** (for garnish)
- **Olive oil** (for brushing)

Instructions:

1. Preheat oven to 475°F (245°C).
2. Roll out the pizza dough and transfer to a baking sheet or pizza stone.
3. Brush the dough lightly with olive oil.
4. Spread cream cheese evenly over the dough.
5. Sprinkle mozzarella cheese on top.
6. Arrange cucumber slices and fresh dill on the pizza.
7. Bake for 10-12 minutes until the cheese is melted and the crust is golden.
8. After baking, garnish with lemon zest and serve.

BBQ Brisket Pizza

Ingredients:

- **1 pizza dough** (store-bought or homemade)
- **1/2 cup BBQ sauce**
- **1 cup mozzarella cheese**, shredded
- **1/2 cup cooked brisket**, shredded
- **1/4 cup red onion**, thinly sliced
- **1/4 cup cilantro**, chopped
- **Fresh jalapeños**, sliced (optional)
- **Olive oil** (for brushing)

Instructions:

1. Preheat oven to 475°F (245°C).
2. Roll out the pizza dough and transfer to a baking sheet or pizza stone.
3. Brush the dough with olive oil.
4. Spread BBQ sauce evenly over the dough.
5. Sprinkle mozzarella cheese over the sauce.
6. Top with shredded brisket, red onion, and jalapeños (if using).
7. Bake for 10-12 minutes until the cheese is melted and the crust is golden.
8. After baking, garnish with fresh cilantro.

Chicken Alfredo Pizza

Ingredients:

- **1 pizza dough** (store-bought or homemade)
- **1/2 cup Alfredo sauce**
- **1/2 cup mozzarella cheese**, shredded
- **1/2 cup cooked chicken**, sliced
- **1/4 cup spinach**, chopped
- **1/4 cup Parmesan cheese**, grated
- **Olive oil** (for brushing)

Instructions:

1. Preheat oven to 475°F (245°C).
2. Roll out the pizza dough and transfer to a baking sheet or pizza stone.
3. Brush the dough with olive oil.
4. Spread Alfredo sauce evenly over the dough.
5. Sprinkle mozzarella cheese and Parmesan cheese over the sauce.
6. Add chicken slices and chopped spinach on top.
7. Bake for 10-12 minutes until the cheese is melted and the crust is golden.

Butternut Squash and Sage Pizza

Ingredients:

- **1 pizza dough** (store-bought or homemade)
- **1/2 cup ricotta cheese**
- **1/2 cup mozzarella cheese**, shredded
- **1 cup butternut squash**, peeled and sliced thinly
- **1/4 cup fresh sage leaves**, chopped
- **Olive oil** (for brushing)
- **Salt and pepper** (to taste)

Instructions:

1. Preheat oven to 475°F (245°C).
2. Roll out the pizza dough and transfer to a baking sheet or pizza stone.
3. Brush the dough with olive oil.
4. Spread ricotta cheese evenly over the dough.
5. Sprinkle mozzarella cheese on top.
6. Add butternut squash slices and fresh sage leaves.
7. Bake for 12-15 minutes until the cheese is melted and the squash is tender.
8. Season with salt and pepper before serving.

Apple and Bacon Pizza

Ingredients:

- **1 pizza dough** (store-bought or homemade)
- **1/2 cup mozzarella cheese**, shredded
- **1/4 cup cheddar cheese**, shredded
- **1/2 cup cooked bacon**, crumbled
- **1 apple**, thinly sliced
- **1/4 cup red onion**, thinly sliced
- **Fresh thyme** (for garnish)
- **Honey** (optional, for drizzling)

Instructions:

1. Preheat oven to 475°F (245°C).
2. Roll out the pizza dough and transfer to a baking sheet or pizza stone.
3. Spread mozzarella and cheddar cheese over the dough.
4. Add crumbled bacon, apple slices, and red onion on top.
5. Bake for 10-12 minutes until the cheese is melted and the crust is golden.
6. After baking, garnish with fresh thyme and drizzle with honey if desired.

Black Bean and Corn Pizza

Ingredients:

- **1 pizza dough** (store-bought or homemade)
- **1/2 cup salsa** (or enchilada sauce)
- **1/2 cup mozzarella cheese**, shredded
- **1/2 cup black beans**, drained and rinsed
- **1/2 cup corn kernels**
- **1/4 cup red onion**, thinly sliced
- **1/4 cup cilantro**, chopped
- **1/4 cup jalapeños**, sliced (optional)
- **Olive oil** (for brushing)

Instructions:

1. Preheat oven to 475°F (245°C).
2. Roll out the pizza dough and transfer to a baking sheet or pizza stone.
3. Brush the dough with olive oil.
4. Spread salsa or enchilada sauce evenly over the dough.
5. Sprinkle mozzarella cheese on top.
6. Add black beans, corn, red onion, and jalapeños (if using) on top.
7. Bake for 10-12 minutes until the cheese is melted and the crust is golden.
8. After baking, garnish with fresh cilantro.

Caramelized Onion and Brie Pizza

Ingredients:

- **1 pizza dough** (store-bought or homemade)
- **1/2 cup caramelized onions** (see instructions below)
- **1/2 cup Brie cheese**, sliced
- **1/4 cup mozzarella cheese**, shredded
- **Fresh thyme** (for garnish)
- **Olive oil** (for brushing)

For Caramelized Onions:

- **2 large onions**, thinly sliced
- **1 tbsp olive oil**
- **1 tsp sugar**
- **Salt and pepper** (to taste)

Instructions:

1. To make caramelized onions: Heat olive oil in a pan over medium heat. Add onions, sugar, salt, and pepper. Cook, stirring occasionally, until the onions are soft and golden brown (about 25 minutes).
2. Preheat oven to 475°F (245°C).
3. Roll out the pizza dough and transfer to a baking sheet or pizza stone.
4. Brush the dough with olive oil.
5. Spread caramelized onions over the dough.
6. Add Brie cheese slices and mozzarella cheese.
7. Bake for 10-12 minutes until the cheese is melted and the crust is golden.
8. After baking, garnish with fresh thyme.

Blue Cheese and Pear Pizza

Ingredients:

- **1 pizza dough** (store-bought or homemade)
- **1/2 cup mozzarella cheese**, shredded
- **1/4 cup blue cheese**, crumbled
- **1 pear**, thinly sliced
- **1/4 cup walnuts**, chopped
- **1/4 cup fresh arugula** (for topping after baking)
- **Balsamic glaze** (optional, for drizzling)

Instructions:

1. Preheat oven to 475°F (245°C).
2. Roll out the pizza dough and transfer to a baking sheet or pizza stone.
3. Brush the dough with olive oil (optional).
4. Sprinkle mozzarella and blue cheese over the dough.
5. Arrange pear slices and chopped walnuts on top.
6. Bake for 10-12 minutes until the cheese is melted and the crust is golden.
7. After baking, top with fresh arugula and drizzle with balsamic glaze.